50 Coffee Recipes for Home

By: Kelly Johnson

Table of Contents

Classic Coffee Recipes:

- Black Coffee
- Americano
- Espresso
- Macchiato
- Café Latte
- Cappuccino
- Flat White
- Café au Lait
- Mocha
- Affogato

Cold Brew and Iced Coffee:

- Cold Brew
- Iced Americano
- Vietnamese Iced Coffee
- Iced Latte
- Caramel Iced Coffee
- Cold Brew Tonic
- Iced Mocha
- Coconut Cold Brew
- Peppermint Mocha Frappuccino
- Iced Cinnamon Almond Milk Macchiato

Flavored and Speciality Coffees:

- Vanilla Latte
- Hazelnut Cappuccino
- Toasted Marshmallow Coffee
- Maple Pecan Latte
- Irish Coffee
- Chocolate Raspberry Mocha
- Gingerbread Latte

- Almond Joy Coffee
- Chai Latte
- Turmeric Golden Latte

Unique Coffee Creations:

- Espresso Tonic with Lavender
- Black and White Russian Coffee
- Cardamom Rose Latte
- Honey Lavender Cold Brew
- Orange Spice Espresso
- Rosemary Infused Coffee
- Cherry Almond Coffee
- Horchata Coffee
- Coconut Lavender Latte
- Spicy Mexican Mocha

Dessert-Inspired Coffees:

- Tiramisu Latte
- Chocolate Cheesecake Coffee
- Crème Brûlée Coffee
- Pumpkin Spice Latte
- Chocolate Covered Strawberry Coffee
- Bananas Foster Coffee
- Salted Caramel Affogato
- Cinnamon Roll Latte
- Blueberry Cobbler Coffee
- Eggnog Latte

Classic Coffee Recipes:

Black Coffee

Ingredients:

- Freshly ground coffee beans
- Hot water

Instructions:

Start by selecting high-quality, freshly roasted coffee beans. Grind the coffee to a medium-coarse consistency for most brewing methods.
Measure the coffee grounds based on your preferred strength, typically using one to two tablespoons of coffee per six ounces of water.
Boil water and let it cool slightly for a moment to around 200°F (93°C). This temperature helps extract flavors without burning the coffee.
Place the coffee grounds in your chosen brewing apparatus, such as a drip coffee maker, French press, pour-over cone, or espresso machine.
Pour the hot water evenly over the coffee grounds, ensuring all grounds are saturated. Let the coffee steep or brew according to your chosen method.
For a drip coffee maker, follow the machine's instructions. For a French press, let it steep for about 4 minutes before pressing down the plunger. For pour-over, slowly pour water in a circular motion over the grounds.
Once brewed, pour the black coffee into your favorite mug, and enjoy it as is or customize it with sugar, cream, or any other preferred additions.

Remember, the key to a great cup of black coffee is using fresh, quality beans, proper brewing equipment, and experimenting with the grind size and water-to-coffee ratio to find your ideal strength and flavor profile.

Americano

Ingredients:

- Freshly ground coffee beans
- Hot water

Instructions:

Begin by brewing a shot of espresso using an espresso machine. The standard serving size is about 1 ounce.
Heat water separately until it's near boiling, typically around 200°F (93°C).
In a separate cup or mug, add the brewed espresso.
Pour hot water over the espresso, adjusting the ratio to your taste preference. A common ratio is 1:1 (equal parts espresso and hot water) or 1:2 for a milder taste.
Stir the espresso and hot water mixture to ensure even distribution.
Taste the Americano and adjust the water-to-espresso ratio as desired.
Serve hot and enjoy the smooth, rich flavor of an Americano.

The Americano is known for its simplicity and ability to resemble drip coffee while maintaining the distinct characteristics of espresso. Adjusting the water-to-espresso ratio allows you to tailor the strength of the Americano to your liking.

Espresso

Ingredients:

- Freshly ground espresso beans

Equipment:

- Espresso machine

Instructions:

Start by choosing high-quality, freshly roasted espresso beans. The grind should be fine, almost like powdered sugar.
Preheat your espresso machine by running a shot of hot water through it.
Measure the espresso grounds, typically using a dose of 7-9 grams for a single shot or 14-18 grams for a double shot.
Tamp the coffee grounds evenly in the portafilter using about 30 pounds of pressure to create a smooth, level surface.
Insert the portafilter into the machine's group head and start the extraction process.
Espresso is brewed under high pressure, usually around 9 bars, forcing hot water through the tamped coffee grounds.
A single shot of espresso typically takes about 25-30 seconds to brew. Adjust the grind size, dose, or extraction time to achieve the desired result.
Once brewed, the espresso should have a thick, golden-brown crema on top.

Enjoy the intense and concentrated flavors of espresso as is or use it as the base for various coffee beverages like lattes, cappuccinos, or Americanos. The key to a good espresso is using fresh, high-quality beans, proper grinding, and precise extraction.

Macchiato

Ingredients:

- Freshly ground espresso beans
- A small amount of milk or foam

Equipment:

- Espresso machine
- Steam wand or milk frother

Instructions:

Begin by preparing a shot of espresso using an espresso machine. A standard single shot is approximately 1 ounce.
Steam a small amount of milk using the steam wand or a milk frother until it reaches a velvety microfoam consistency.
Pour the shot of espresso into a small espresso cup or glass.
Spoon a small amount of the frothed milk or foam on top of the espresso. The purpose is to "stain" the espresso, giving it a touch of creaminess.
The milk in a macchiato is minimal, creating a strong coffee flavor with a hint of milk.

There are variations of macchiatos, including caramel or vanilla macchiatos, where flavored syrups are added for extra sweetness. However, the classic macchiato is a simple and elegant coffee beverage that highlights the boldness of espresso with just a hint of milk.

Café Latte

Ingredients:

- Freshly ground espresso beans
- Steamed milk

Equipment:

- Espresso machine
- Steam wand

Instructions:

Start by brewing a shot of espresso using an espresso machine. A standard single shot is approximately 1 ounce.
Steam the milk using the steam wand until it reaches a creamy and velvety microfoam consistency. Ensure not to overheat the milk.
Pour the shot of espresso into a latte glass or cup.
Gently pour the steamed milk over the espresso, holding back the foam with a spoon to create a layered effect.
Add a small amount of the milk foam on top to finish.

The ratio of espresso to steamed milk in a latte is typically around 1:2, but you can adjust it based on your preference. A latte is known for its smooth and creamy texture, making it a popular and versatile coffee beverage. You can also add flavored syrups like vanilla or caramel to customize the taste.

Cappuccino

Ingredients:

- Freshly ground espresso beans
- Steamed milk
- Foam

Equipment:

- Espresso machine
- Steam wand

Instructions:

> Begin by brewing a shot of espresso using an espresso machine. A standard single shot is approximately 1 ounce.
> Steam the milk using the steam wand until it reaches a velvety microfoam consistency.
> Pour the shot of espresso into a cappuccino cup.
> Gently pour the steamed milk over the espresso, holding back the foam with a spoon to create a layered effect. Aim for a 1:1:1 ratio of espresso, steamed milk, and foam.
> Finish by spooning the foam on top of the steamed milk.

A classic cappuccino is known for its equal parts of espresso, steamed milk, and foam, creating a rich and creamy texture. The balance between the three components is crucial, giving the cappuccino its signature taste and mouthfeel. Adjust the ratio based on your preference, and feel free to add a sprinkle of cocoa or cinnamon on top for extra flavor.

Flat White

Ingredients:

- Freshly ground espresso beans
- Steamed microfoam

Equipment:

- Espresso machine
- Steam wand

Instructions:

Start by brewing a double shot of espresso using an espresso machine. A standard double shot is approximately 2 ounces.

Steam the milk using the steam wand to create a velvety microfoam. The goal is to achieve a smooth, glossy texture without large bubbles.

Pour the double shot of espresso into a flat white cup or glass.

Gently pour the steamed microfoam over the espresso, creating a thin layer of foam on top. Aim for a higher coffee-to-milk ratio compared to a latte or cappuccino, but less foam than a cappuccino.

The result should be a coffee beverage with a strong and bold flavor, complemented by the creamy texture of the microfoam.

The flat white originated in Australia and New Zealand and has gained popularity worldwide for its balance of strong espresso and silky microfoam. The emphasis is on the coffee flavor, with the microfoam providing a smooth and velvety mouthfeel. Adjust the ratios based on personal preference for a stronger or milder taste.

Café au Lait

Ingredients:

- Freshly ground coffee beans
- Equal parts brewed coffee and steamed milk

Equipment:

- Coffee maker
- Steam wand (optional)

Instructions:

Brew a strong cup of coffee using your preferred method, such as a drip coffee maker, pour-over, or French press.
While the coffee is brewing, heat an equal amount of milk until it's hot but not boiling. You can heat the milk on the stove or use a steam wand if available.
Once the coffee is brewed and the milk is heated, pour the brewed coffee into a large mug.
Slowly pour the hot milk into the coffee, ensuring an even distribution.
Stir the coffee and milk together to combine.

Café au Lait, which translates to "coffee with milk" in French, is a simple and comforting beverage. It differs from a latte in that it typically uses brewed coffee instead of espresso, and the coffee-to-milk ratio is equal. Adjust the strength by varying the coffee's brewing method and the type of milk used.

Mocha

Ingredients:

- Freshly ground espresso beans or strong brewed coffee
- Cocoa powder or chocolate syrup
- Steamed milk
- Whipped cream (optional)
- Chocolate shavings or cocoa powder for garnish (optional)

Equipment:

- Espresso machine (or coffee maker for strong brewed coffee)
- Steam wand
- Whisk (if using cocoa powder)

Instructions:

Brew a double shot of espresso using an espresso machine, or prepare a cup of strong brewed coffee.

In a small bowl, mix 1-2 tablespoons of cocoa powder with a small amount of hot water to create a smooth chocolate paste. Alternatively, use chocolate syrup.

Pour the chocolate paste or syrup into the bottom of a coffee mug.

Brew the espresso directly over the chocolate, stirring to combine. If using brewed coffee, add it to the chocolate and stir.

Steam milk using the steam wand until it reaches a velvety microfoam consistency.

Pour the steamed milk over the chocolate and espresso mixture, holding back the foam with a spoon.

Spoon the remaining foam on top of the mocha.

Optionally, add whipped cream on top and garnish with chocolate shavings or a sprinkle of cocoa powder.

A mocha is a delightful combination of rich chocolate and bold coffee, creating a comforting and indulgent drink. Adjust the sweetness and chocolate intensity to suit your taste preferences. Enjoy the mocha as a special treat or dessert-like coffee beverage.

Affogato

Ingredients:

- Vanilla ice cream or gelato
- A shot of freshly brewed espresso

Equipment:

- Espresso machine

Instructions:

> Place a scoop of vanilla ice cream or gelato in a serving glass or cup.
> Brew a shot of espresso using an espresso machine directly over the ice cream.
> Allow the hot espresso to melt and blend with the cold ice cream.
> Serve immediately, capturing the contrast between the hot espresso and the cold, creamy ice cream.

Affogato, which means "drowned" in Italian, is a simple and elegant dessert-like coffee treat. The hot espresso melts the ice cream, creating a delightful blend of creamy, cold sweetness and bold, hot coffee. Customize it by trying different flavors of ice cream or adding a sprinkle of cocoa powder or a drizzle of caramel for extra flair. Enjoy this quick and satisfying coffee indulgence!

Cold Brew and Iced Coffee:

Cold Brew

Ingredients:

- Coarsely ground coffee beans
- Cold or room temperature water

Equipment:

- Coffee grinder
- Cold brew coffee maker or large jar
- Fine mesh sieve or coffee filter
- Optional: Sweeteners, milk, or flavored syrups for serving

Instructions:

Coarsely grind your coffee beans. Use a ratio of about 1 cup of coarsely ground coffee to 4 cups of water. Adjust according to your taste preference and the strength you desire.
In a cold brew coffee maker or a large jar, combine the coarsely ground coffee with cold or room temperature water.
Stir the mixture well, ensuring that all the coffee grounds are fully saturated.
Seal the container and let it steep in the refrigerator for at least 12-24 hours. A longer steeping time will result in a stronger concentrate.
After steeping, strain the cold brew concentrate using a fine mesh sieve, coffee filter, or a cold brew coffee maker to remove the coffee grounds.
Dilute the concentrated cold brew with water or milk to your desired strength. A common ratio is 1 part concentrate to 1-2 parts water or milk.
Serve the cold brew over ice and customize with sweeteners, milk, or flavored syrups if desired.

Cold brew is known for its smooth, mellow flavor with lower acidity compared to hot-brewed coffee. It's a refreshing and versatile beverage, perfect for hot days or as a base for various coffee creations.

Iced Americano

Ingredients:

- Freshly ground coffee beans
- Ice cubes
- Cold water

Equipment:

- Espresso machine (or strong brewed coffee)
- Glass or cup
- Ice maker

Instructions:

Brew a double shot of espresso using an espresso machine. A standard double shot is approximately 2 ounces.
- If you don't have an espresso machine, you can make a strong cup of coffee using your preferred brewing method. It should be about 4 ounces of strong coffee.

Fill a glass or cup with ice cubes.
Pour the freshly brewed espresso or strong coffee over the ice.
Optionally, add cold water to adjust the strength and dilute the coffee to your preference.
Stir the iced Americano to ensure even distribution of the coffee and chill it further.
Customize your iced Americano with sweeteners, flavored syrups, or a splash of milk if desired.

Iced Americano is a simple and refreshing coffee drink that combines the boldness of espresso with the coolness of ice. It's a great choice for those who enjoy a milder coffee flavor in a chilled form.

Vietnamese Iced Coffee

Ingredients:

- Coarsely ground dark roast coffee (preferably Vietnamese coffee)
- Sweetened condensed milk
- Ice cubes

Equipment:

- Vietnamese drip coffee maker (phin) or a drip coffee maker
- Glass or cup

Instructions:

Place 2-3 tablespoons of coarsely ground coffee into the Vietnamese drip coffee maker (phin).
- If using a drip coffee maker, use a filter and set it up according to your machine's instructions.

Place the phin or drip coffee maker over a glass.

Pour a small amount of hot water (just off boiling) over the coffee grounds to allow them to bloom. Wait for about 20-30 seconds.

Add more hot water to the phin or start your drip coffee maker. Allow the coffee to slowly drip through.

While the coffee is brewing, add 1-2 tablespoons of sweetened condensed milk to a glass.

Once the coffee has finished brewing, pour it over the sweetened condensed milk. Stir well to combine.

Add ice cubes to the glass to cool the coffee and create the classic iced coffee experience.

Stir again and enjoy your Vietnamese Iced Coffee!

Vietnamese Iced Coffee, or "cà phê sữa đá," is a delightful combination of strong, dark coffee and the sweet creaminess of condensed milk. Adjust the amount of sweetened condensed milk to your liking, and savor the unique flavors of this traditional Vietnamese coffee.

Iced Latte

Ingredients:

- Freshly ground espresso beans (or strong brewed coffee)
- Cold milk
- Ice cubes

Equipment:

- Espresso machine (or coffee maker for strong brewed coffee)
- Glass or cup

Instructions:

Brew a double shot of espresso using an espresso machine. A standard double shot is approximately 2 ounces.
- If you don't have an espresso machine, you can make a strong cup of coffee using your preferred brewing method. It should be about 4 ounces of strong coffee.

Fill a glass with ice cubes.
Pour the freshly brewed espresso or strong coffee over the ice.
Add cold milk to the glass, leaving room for customization based on your taste preference.
Stir well to combine the coffee, milk, and ice.
Customize your iced latte by adding sweeteners, flavored syrups, or a splash of vanilla extract if desired.
Optionally, top your iced latte with whipped cream or a sprinkle of cocoa for added indulgence.

Iced lattes offer a refreshing and creamy coffee experience, combining the richness of espresso with cold milk and ice. Feel free to experiment with milk alternatives like almond, soy, or oat milk for different flavor profiles.

Caramel Iced Coffee

Ingredients:

- Freshly ground coffee beans (or strong brewed coffee)
- Cold milk
- Ice cubes
- Caramel syrup
- Whipped cream (optional)
- Caramel drizzle (optional)

Equipment:

- Espresso machine (or coffee maker for strong brewed coffee)
- Glass or cup

Instructions:

Brew a double shot of espresso using an espresso machine. A standard double shot is approximately 2 ounces.
- If you don't have an espresso machine, you can make a strong cup of coffee using your preferred brewing method. It should be about 4 ounces of strong coffee.

Fill a glass with ice cubes.
Pour the freshly brewed espresso or strong coffee over the ice.
Add cold milk to the glass, leaving room for customization based on your taste preference.
Add caramel syrup to the coffee and stir well to combine. Start with 1-2 tablespoons and adjust according to your sweetness preference.
Optionally, top your caramel iced coffee with whipped cream.
Drizzle additional caramel syrup on top for extra flavor and presentation.
Stir once more before enjoying your delicious caramel iced coffee.

Caramel iced coffee is a delightful and indulgent treat, combining the boldness of coffee with the sweetness of caramel. Customize the sweetness level and add your favorite toppings for a personalized experience.

Cold Brew Tonic

Ingredients:

- Cold brew concentrate
- Tonic water
- Ice cubes
- Lemon or orange wedge (for garnish, optional)
- Simple syrup (optional, for sweetness)

Equipment:

- Tall glass

Instructions:

Fill a tall glass with ice cubes.
Pour cold brew concentrate into the glass, leaving room for the tonic water.
Top the cold brew with tonic water, adjusting the ratio based on your preference.
A common ratio is 1:1 or 1:2 (cold brew to tonic water).
Stir gently to mix the cold brew and tonic water.
Optionally, add simple syrup to sweeten the drink. Start with a small amount and adjust to taste.
Garnish with a lemon or orange wedge if desired.
Stir again before sipping to ensure the flavors are well combined.

Cold Brew Tonic is a refreshing and effervescent beverage that combines the smoothness of cold brew coffee with the bubbles of tonic water. The result is a light and crisp drink that's perfect for warm days or as a unique alternative to traditional coffee preparations. Adjust the sweetness and citrus elements to suit your taste preferences.

Iced Mocha

Ingredients:

- Freshly ground espresso beans (or strong brewed coffee)
- Cocoa powder or chocolate syrup
- Cold milk
- Ice cubes
- Whipped cream (optional)
- Chocolate shavings or cocoa powder for garnish (optional)

Equipment:

- Espresso machine (or coffee maker for strong brewed coffee)
- Glass or cup

Instructions:

Brew a double shot of espresso using an espresso machine. A standard double shot is approximately 2 ounces.
- If you don't have an espresso machine, you can make a strong cup of coffee using your preferred brewing method. It should be about 4 ounces of strong coffee.

Fill a glass with ice cubes.
In a small bowl, mix 1-2 tablespoons of cocoa powder with a small amount of hot water to create a smooth chocolate paste. Alternatively, use chocolate syrup.
Pour the chocolate paste or syrup into the freshly brewed espresso or strong coffee. Stir well to combine.
Add cold milk to the glass, leaving room for customization based on your taste preference.
Stir the mixture well to combine the coffee, chocolate, and milk.
Optionally, top your iced mocha with whipped cream and garnish with chocolate shavings or a sprinkle of cocoa powder.
Stir once more before enjoying your delicious iced mocha.

Iced mochas offer a perfect blend of rich chocolate and bold coffee flavors, served over ice for a refreshing treat. Customize the sweetness, chocolate intensity, and toppings to suit your preferences.

Coconut Cold Brew

Ingredients:

- Coarsely ground coffee beans
- Cold water
- Coconut milk (canned or carton)
- Ice cubes
- Sweetener of choice (optional)
- Shredded coconut for garnish (optional)

Equipment:

- Cold brew coffee maker or large jar
- Fine mesh sieve or coffee filter
- Glass or cup

Instructions:

Coarsely grind your coffee beans. Use a ratio of about 1 cup of coarsely ground coffee to 4 cups of cold water. Adjust according to your taste preference and the strength you desire.
In a cold brew coffee maker or a large jar, combine the coarsely ground coffee with cold water.
Stir the mixture well, ensuring that all the coffee grounds are fully saturated.
Seal the container and let it steep in the refrigerator for at least 12-24 hours. A longer steeping time will result in a stronger concentrate.
After steeping, strain the cold brew concentrate using a fine mesh sieve, coffee filter, or a cold brew coffee maker to remove the coffee grounds.
Fill a glass with ice cubes.
Pour the cold brew concentrate over the ice.
Add coconut milk to the glass, leaving room for customization based on your taste preference.
Optionally, add sweetener if desired and stir well.
Garnish with shredded coconut on top if you like.

Coconut Cold Brew offers a tropical twist to the classic cold brew, with the creamy and nutty flavor of coconut milk. Adjust the coconut milk ratio and sweetness to suit your taste preferences, and enjoy a refreshing and exotic iced coffee.

Peppermint Mocha Frappuccino

Ingredients:

- Freshly brewed espresso or strong coffee, chilled
- Ice cubes
- Milk (dairy or non-dairy)
- Chocolate syrup
- Peppermint extract or peppermint syrup
- Whipped cream
- Crushed peppermint candies or chocolate shavings for garnish (optional)

Equipment:

- Blender
- Glass or cup

Instructions:

Brew a double shot of espresso or make a strong cup of coffee. Allow it to cool and chill in the refrigerator.
Fill a blender with ice cubes.
Pour the chilled espresso or strong coffee over the ice in the blender.
Add milk to the blender, adjusting the amount based on your desired thickness and creaminess.
Add 2-3 tablespoons of chocolate syrup to the blender.
Add 1/4 to 1/2 teaspoon of peppermint extract or 1-2 pumps of peppermint syrup to the blender. Adjust to your preferred level of minty flavor.
Blend the mixture until smooth and creamy.
Pour the Peppermint Mocha Frappuccino into a glass.
Top with whipped cream and garnish with crushed peppermint candies or chocolate shavings if desired.
Optionally, drizzle additional chocolate syrup over the whipped cream for extra indulgence.

Enjoy the refreshing and festive Peppermint Mocha Frappuccino as a delightful treat, especially during the holiday season. Adjust the sweetness and mint flavor to suit your taste preferences.

Iced Cinnamon Almond Milk Macchiato

Ingredients:

- Freshly brewed espresso or strong coffee, chilled
- Ice cubes
- Almond milk (sweetened or unsweetened)
- Cinnamon syrup or ground cinnamon
- Vanilla extract (optional)
- Sweetener of choice (optional)

Equipment:

- Glass or cup
- Stirring stick or spoon

Instructions:

Brew a double shot of espresso or make a strong cup of coffee. Allow it to cool and chill in the refrigerator.
Fill a glass with ice cubes.
Pour the chilled espresso or strong coffee over the ice in the glass.
In a separate container, froth or heat a desired amount of almond milk. If using sweetened almond milk, you may adjust the sweetness level accordingly.
Slowly pour the frothed or heated almond milk over the coffee and ice. Hold back the foam with a spoon to create a layered effect.
Optionally, add vanilla extract to the almond milk for additional flavor.
Drizzle cinnamon syrup over the top of the almond milk or sprinkle ground cinnamon.
Optionally, add sweetener to the entire drink and stir well.
Stir the layers gently to combine the flavors.
Enjoy your Iced Cinnamon Almond Milk Macchiato!

This delightful drink combines the nutty flavor of almond milk with the richness of coffee and a hint of cinnamon. Customize the sweetness and cinnamon intensity to suit your taste preferences for a refreshing and aromatic beverage.

Flavored and Speciality Coffees:

Vanilla Latte

Ingredients:

- Freshly ground espresso beans (or strong brewed coffee)
- Milk (dairy or non-dairy)
- Vanilla syrup or vanilla extract
- Optional: Sweetener of choice
- Optional: Whipped cream for topping

Equipment:

- Espresso machine (or coffee maker for strong brewed coffee)
- Steam wand (if using an espresso machine)
- Glass or cup

Instructions:

Brew a double shot of espresso using an espresso machine. A standard double shot is approximately 2 ounces.
- If you don't have an espresso machine, you can make a strong cup of coffee using your preferred brewing method. It should be about 4 ounces of strong coffee.

In a separate container, heat and froth the milk. If using an espresso machine, use the steam wand to create velvety microfoam. If not, heat the milk on the stove and use a handheld frother or whisk for frothing.

Add vanilla syrup or vanilla extract to the freshly brewed espresso or strong coffee. Start with 1-2 tablespoons of syrup or a few drops of extract, adjusting to your taste preference.

Optionally, add sweetener to the coffee if desired.

Pour the frothed milk over the coffee, holding back the foam with a spoon to create a layered effect.

Stir gently to combine the coffee, vanilla, and milk.

Optionally, top the Vanilla Latte with whipped cream for an extra indulgent touch.

Serve and enjoy your delicious Vanilla Latte!

The Vanilla Latte is a classic and comforting coffee drink, combining the warmth of espresso, the sweetness of vanilla, and the creamy texture of frothed milk. Adjust the sweetness and vanilla intensity to suit your taste.

Hazelnut Cappuccino

Ingredients:

- Freshly ground espresso beans
- Milk (dairy or non-dairy)
- Hazelnut syrup or hazelnut-flavored coffee syrup
- Optional: Sweetener of choice
- Optional: Crushed hazelnuts for garnish

Equipment:

- Espresso machine
- Steam wand
- Cappuccino cup or glass

Instructions:

Brew a double shot of espresso using an espresso machine. A standard double shot is approximately 2 ounces.
In a separate container, heat and froth the milk using the steam wand of the espresso machine. Create velvety microfoam for a cappuccino.
Add hazelnut syrup or hazelnut-flavored coffee syrup to the freshly brewed espresso. Start with 1-2 tablespoons of syrup, adjusting to your taste preference.
Optionally, add sweetener to the coffee if desired.
Pour the frothed milk over the hazelnut-infused espresso, holding back the foam with a spoon to create a layered effect.
Spoon the remaining foam on top of the cappuccino, creating a creamy and textured surface.
Optionally, garnish the Hazelnut Cappuccino with crushed hazelnuts for added flavor and presentation.
Serve immediately and enjoy your delicious Hazelnut Cappuccino!

This Hazelnut Cappuccino combines the rich and nutty flavor of hazelnut with the boldness of espresso, creating a delightful and aromatic coffee experience. Adjust the sweetness and hazelnut intensity to suit your taste preferences.

Toasted Marshmallow Coffee

Ingredients:

- Freshly brewed coffee
- Milk (dairy or non-dairy)
- Marshmallow syrup or marshmallow-flavored coffee syrup
- Toasted marshmallows for garnish
- Optional: Sweetener of choice
- Optional: Whipped cream for topping

Equipment:

- Coffee maker
- Milk frother (optional)
- Mug or cup

Instructions:

Brew your favorite coffee using a coffee maker. Prepare a strong cup of coffee, adjusting the amount based on your preferred coffee-to-milk ratio.

In a separate container, heat and froth the milk using a milk frother or by heating on the stove and whisking manually. Aim for velvety microfoam for a creamy texture.

Add marshmallow syrup or marshmallow-flavored coffee syrup to the freshly brewed coffee. Start with 1-2 tablespoons of syrup, adjusting to your taste preference.

Optionally, add sweetener to the coffee if desired.

Pour the frothed milk over the marshmallow-infused coffee, holding back the foam with a spoon to create a layered effect.

Stir gently to combine the coffee, marshmallow, and milk.

Optionally, top the Toasted Marshmallow Coffee with whipped cream for added richness.

Garnish with toasted marshmallows on top for a delightful finishing touch.

Serve and enjoy your Toasted Marshmallow Coffee!

This creative coffee variation captures the essence of toasted marshmallows, providing a comforting and sweet flavor profile. Adjust the sweetness and marshmallow intensity to suit your taste preferences for a cozy and indulgent coffee experience.

Maple Pecan Latte

Ingredients:

- Freshly brewed espresso or strong coffee
- Milk (dairy or non-dairy)
- Maple syrup
- Pecan-flavored syrup or pecan extract
- Chopped pecans for garnish
- Optional: Sweetener of choice
- Optional: Whipped cream for topping

Equipment:

- Espresso machine (or coffee maker for strong brewed coffee)
- Steam wand
- Latte glass or cup

Instructions:

Brew a double shot of espresso using an espresso machine. A standard double shot is approximately 2 ounces.
- If you don't have an espresso machine, you can make a strong cup of coffee using your preferred brewing method. It should be about 4 ounces of strong coffee.

In a separate container, heat and froth the milk using the steam wand of the espresso machine. Create velvety microfoam for a latte.

Add maple syrup to the freshly brewed espresso or strong coffee. Start with 1-2 tablespoons of syrup, adjusting to your taste preference.

Add pecan-flavored syrup or a few drops of pecan extract to the coffee. Start with 1-2 tablespoons of syrup, adjusting to your taste preference.

Optionally, add sweetener to the coffee if desired.

Pour the frothed milk over the maple-pecan infused espresso, holding back the foam with a spoon to create a layered effect.

Stir gently to combine the coffee, maple, pecan, and milk.

Optionally, top the Maple Pecan Latte with whipped cream.

Garnish with chopped pecans on top for added flavor and presentation.

Serve and enjoy your Maple Pecan Latte!

This delightful latte combines the warmth of maple, the nutty richness of pecans, and the boldness of coffee for a comforting and flavorful experience. Adjust the sweetness and maple-pecan intensity to suit your taste preferences.

Irish Coffee

Ingredients:

- Freshly brewed hot coffee
- Irish whiskey
- Brown sugar (or sugar cube)
- Heavy cream

Equipment:

- Irish coffee mug or heat-resistant glass
- Spoon
- Handheld milk frother (optional)

Instructions:

Brew a strong cup of hot coffee using your preferred brewing method.
While the coffee is brewing, warm the Irish coffee mug or glass by filling it with hot water. Let it sit for a minute, then discard the water.
Pour the freshly brewed coffee into the warm mug or glass, leaving some space at the top.
Add brown sugar or a sugar cube to the coffee. Adjust the amount based on your sweetness preference.
Stir well until the sugar is dissolved in the hot coffee.
Pour a shot (about 1.5 ounces) of Irish whiskey into the coffee. Adjust the amount to your liking.
In a separate container, slightly whip the heavy cream until it thickens but is still pourable. You can use a handheld milk frother or simply whisk by hand.
Gently pour the whipped heavy cream over the back of a spoon to let it float on top of the coffee. The cream should sit atop the coffee without fully mixing.
Optionally, garnish with a sprinkle of cocoa powder or nutmeg on top of the cream.
Serve immediately and enjoy your classic Irish Coffee!

Irish Coffee is a warm and inviting cocktail that combines the robust flavor of coffee with the richness of Irish whiskey and the creaminess of whipped cream. Adjust the whiskey and sugar levels to suit your taste preferences.

Chocolate Raspberry Mocha

Ingredients:

- Freshly brewed espresso or strong coffee
- Cocoa powder or chocolate syrup
- Raspberry syrup
- Milk (dairy or non-dairy)
- Whipped cream
- Fresh raspberries for garnish (optional)
- Chocolate shavings for garnish (optional)

Equipment:

- Espresso machine (or coffee maker for strong brewed coffee)
- Steam wand (if using an espresso machine)
- Mocha cup or glass

Instructions:

Brew a double shot of espresso using an espresso machine. A standard double shot is approximately 2 ounces.
- If you don't have an espresso machine, you can make a strong cup of coffee using your preferred brewing method. It should be about 4 ounces of strong coffee.

In a small bowl, mix 1-2 tablespoons of cocoa powder with a small amount of hot water to create a smooth chocolate paste. Alternatively, use chocolate syrup.
Pour the chocolate paste or syrup into the freshly brewed espresso or strong coffee. Stir well to combine.
Add raspberry syrup to the mocha. Start with 1-2 tablespoons of syrup, adjusting to your taste preference.
In a separate container, heat and froth the milk using the steam wand of the espresso machine. Create velvety microfoam for a creamy texture.
Pour the frothed milk over the chocolate-raspberry-infused espresso, holding back the foam with a spoon to create a layered effect.
Stir gently to combine the mocha, raspberry, and milk.
Optionally, top the Chocolate Raspberry Mocha with whipped cream.
Garnish with fresh raspberries and chocolate shavings for added flavor and presentation.

Serve immediately and enjoy your indulgent Chocolate Raspberry Mocha!

This delicious variation combines the rich flavors of chocolate and raspberry with the boldness of coffee, creating a delightful and decadent mocha experience. Adjust the sweetness and raspberry-chocolate intensity to suit your taste preferences.

Gingerbread Latte

Ingredients:

- Freshly brewed espresso or strong coffee
- Milk (dairy or non-dairy)
- Gingerbread syrup
- Ground cinnamon
- Ground ginger
- Ground nutmeg
- Optional: Sweetener of choice
- Optional: Whipped cream for topping
- Optional: Crushed gingerbread cookies for garnish

Equipment:

- Espresso machine (or coffee maker for strong brewed coffee)
- Steam wand
- Latte glass or cup

Instructions:

Brew a double shot of espresso using an espresso machine. A standard double shot is approximately 2 ounces.
- If you don't have an espresso machine, you can make a strong cup of coffee using your preferred brewing method. It should be about 4 ounces of strong coffee.

In a small bowl, mix a pinch of ground cinnamon, ground ginger, and ground nutmeg. This will be your gingerbread spice blend.

Pour the freshly brewed espresso or strong coffee into a latte glass or cup.

Add gingerbread syrup to the coffee. Start with 1-2 tablespoons of syrup, adjusting to your taste preference.

Stir in a pinch of the gingerbread spice blend into the coffee.

In a separate container, heat and froth the milk using the steam wand of the espresso machine. Create velvety microfoam for a latte.

Pour the frothed milk over the gingerbread-infused espresso, holding back the foam with a spoon to create a layered effect.

Stir gently to combine the gingerbread, spice, and milk.

Optionally, top the Gingerbread Latte with whipped cream.
Garnish with a sprinkle of the gingerbread spice blend or crushed gingerbread cookies for added flavor and presentation.
Serve immediately and savor the festive and aromatic Gingerbread Latte!

This seasonal favorite captures the warm and spicy flavors of gingerbread, making it a perfect treat for the holiday season. Adjust the sweetness and spice levels to suit your taste preferences.

Almond Joy Coffee

Ingredients:

- Freshly brewed coffee
- Coconut milk (canned or carton)
- Almond syrup or almond extract
- Chocolate syrup
- Shredded coconut
- Optional: Sweetener of choice
- Optional: Whipped cream for topping
- Optional: Almond slices for garnish

Equipment:

- Coffee maker
- Saucepan (if using canned coconut milk)
- Mug or cup

Instructions:

Brew a strong cup of coffee using your preferred brewing method.
In a saucepan, gently heat the coconut milk until it's warm but not boiling. If using canned coconut milk, you may need to stir and mix the creamy part with the liquid part.
Pour the freshly brewed coffee into a mug.
Add almond syrup or a few drops of almond extract to the coffee. Start with 1-2 tablespoons of syrup, adjusting to your taste preference.
Add chocolate syrup to the coffee. Start with 1-2 tablespoons of syrup, adjusting to your taste preference.
Pour the warmed coconut milk into the coffee, holding back the foam with a spoon to create a layered effect.
Stir gently to combine the almond, chocolate, and coconut flavors with the coffee.
Optionally, top the Almond Joy Coffee with whipped cream.
Sprinkle shredded coconut on top for added texture and flavor.
Optionally, garnish with almond slices for a finishing touch.
Serve and enjoy your delicious Almond Joy Coffee!

This coffee variation brings together the classic combination of almonds, chocolate, and coconut, reminiscent of the popular candy bar. Adjust the sweetness and almond-chocolate-coconut intensity to suit your taste preferences.

Chai Latte

Ingredients:

- Chai tea bag or loose chai tea blend
- Water
- Milk (dairy or non-dairy)
- Sweetener of choice (optional)
- Ground cinnamon (optional)
- Ground ginger (optional)
- Ground cardamom (optional)
- Ground cloves (optional)
- Ground nutmeg (optional)

Equipment:

- Saucepan
- Whisk or spoon
- Mug or cup

Instructions:

In a saucepan, heat water until it's hot but not boiling.
Add the chai tea bag or loose chai tea blend to the hot water.
Let the tea steep for about 5-7 minutes, or follow the instructions on the tea packaging for the appropriate steeping time.
While the tea is steeping, heat the milk in the saucepan or using a steam wand until it's warm but not boiling. Froth the milk if desired for a latte-like texture.
Remove the tea bag or strain the loose tea from the steeped chai.
Pour the brewed chai tea into a mug.
Add the warmed milk to the mug, holding back the foam with a spoon to create a layered effect.
Optionally, add sweetener to the chai latte if desired.
Stir gently to combine the tea and milk.
Optionally, sprinkle ground cinnamon, ground ginger, ground cardamom, ground cloves, and ground nutmeg on top for added spice.
Serve and enjoy your comforting Chai Latte!

Chai Latte brings together the aromatic and spiced flavors of chai tea with the creaminess of steamed milk, creating a delightful and warming beverage. Adjust the sweetness and spice levels to suit your taste preferences.

Turmeric Golden Latte

Ingredients:

- Turmeric powder
- Milk (dairy or non-dairy)
- Honey or maple syrup
- Ground cinnamon
- Ground ginger
- Ground black pepper
- Optional: Vanilla extract
- Optional: Coconut oil or ghee for added richness

Equipment:

- Saucepan
- Whisk or spoon
- Mug or cup

Instructions:

In a saucepan, heat the milk until it's warm but not boiling.
Add turmeric powder, ground cinnamon, ground ginger, and a pinch of ground black pepper to the milk. Start with 1/2 teaspoon of turmeric and adjust to your taste preference.
Optionally, add a small amount of vanilla extract for added flavor.
If desired, add a teaspoon of honey or maple syrup to sweeten the golden latte. Adjust the sweetness to your liking.
If using, add a small amount of coconut oil or ghee for added richness. This step is optional but adds creaminess to the latte.
Whisk or stir the ingredients together until the turmeric is fully dissolved, and the mixture is well combined.
Heat the mixture until it's warm, making sure not to boil.
Pour the turmeric golden latte into a mug.
Optionally, sprinkle a bit more ground cinnamon on top for garnish.
Serve and savor the comforting and nourishing Turmeric Golden Latte!

Turmeric Golden Latte, also known as "Golden Milk," combines the anti-inflammatory properties of turmeric with warming spices and a touch of sweetness. Adjust the spice levels and sweetness to suit your taste preferences for a soothing and healthful beverage.

Unique Coffee Creations:

Espresso Tonic with Lavender

Ingredients:

- Double shot of espresso
- Tonic water
- Lavender syrup
- Ice cubes
- Fresh lavender sprig for garnish

Equipment:

- Espresso machine
- Glass or cup
- Stirring stick or spoon

Instructions:

Brew a double shot of espresso using an espresso machine. A standard double shot is approximately 2 ounces.
Fill a glass with ice cubes.
Pour the freshly brewed espresso over the ice in the glass.
Add tonic water to the glass, leaving room for customization based on your taste preference.
Stir gently to combine the espresso and tonic water.
Add lavender syrup to the mixture. Start with 1-2 tablespoons of syrup, adjusting to your taste preference.
Garnish the drink with a fresh lavender sprig for added aroma and presentation.
Stir once more to ensure the lavender syrup is well incorporated.
Serve immediately and enjoy your refreshing Espresso Tonic with Lavender!

This unique coffee creation combines the boldness of espresso with the effervescence of tonic water, enhanced by the floral and aromatic notes of lavender. Adjust the sweetness and lavender intensity to suit your taste preferences for a delightful and invigorating drink.

Black and White Russian Coffee

Ingredients:

- Freshly brewed strong coffee
- Vodka
- Coffee liqueur (e.g., Kahlúa)
- Heavy cream
- Ice cubes
- Chocolate syrup for garnish (optional)

Equipment:

- Mug or glass
- Stirring stick or spoon

Instructions:

Brew a strong cup of coffee using your preferred brewing method.
Fill a glass or mug with ice cubes.
Pour 1 ounce of vodka over the ice.
Add 1 ounce of coffee liqueur to the glass.
Pour the freshly brewed strong coffee over the ice, vodka, and coffee liqueur.
Stir the ingredients together in the glass.
In a separate container, slightly heat the heavy cream. It should be warm but not boiling.
Slowly pour the warm heavy cream over the back of a spoon onto the surface of the coffee, allowing it to float on top. This creates the "white" layer.
Optionally, drizzle chocolate syrup on top for garnish and added flavor.
Serve and enjoy your decadent Black and White Russian Coffee!

This coffee variation is inspired by the classic Black Russian and White Russian cocktails, combining the richness of coffee with the smoothness of vodka and coffee liqueur. The layered presentation adds a visually appealing touch to this indulgent beverage. Adjust the ratios to your liking and savor the delightful flavors.

Cardamom Rose Latte

Ingredients:

- Freshly brewed espresso or strong coffee
- Milk (dairy or non-dairy)
- Cardamom syrup or ground cardamom
- Rose water
- Sweetener of choice (optional)
- Dried rose petals for garnish (optional)

Equipment:

- Espresso machine (or coffee maker for strong brewed coffee)
- Steam wand
- Latte glass or cup

Instructions:

Brew a double shot of espresso using an espresso machine. A standard double shot is approximately 2 ounces.
- If you don't have an espresso machine, you can make a strong cup of coffee using your preferred brewing method. It should be about 4 ounces of strong coffee.

In a separate container, heat and froth the milk using the steam wand of the espresso machine. Create velvety microfoam for a latte.

Add cardamom syrup or a pinch of ground cardamom to the freshly brewed espresso or strong coffee. Start with 1-2 tablespoons of syrup or a pinch of ground cardamom, adjusting to your taste preference.

Add rose water to the coffee. Start with 1-2 teaspoons of rose water, adjusting to your taste preference.

Optionally, add sweetener to the coffee if desired.

Pour the frothed milk over the cardamom-rose-infused espresso, holding back the foam with a spoon to create a layered effect.

Stir gently to combine the cardamom, rose, and milk.

Optionally, top the Cardamom Rose Latte with a sprinkle of dried rose petals for added aroma and presentation.

Serve immediately and enjoy the exotic and fragrant Cardamom Rose Latte!

This unique latte variation combines the warm and aromatic spice of cardamom with the floral notes of rose water, creating a delightful and sophisticated coffee experience. Adjust the sweetness and cardamom-rose intensity to suit your taste preferences.

Honey Lavender Cold Brew

Ingredients:

- Coarsely ground coffee beans (for cold brew)
- Cold or room temperature water
- Lavender syrup
- Honey
- Ice cubes
- Optional: Lavender buds for garnish

Equipment:

- Cold brew coffee maker or jar
- Fine mesh strainer or cheesecloth
- Pitcher
- Stirring stick or spoon
- Glass

Instructions:

Prepare Cold Brew Concentrate:
- Combine coarsely ground coffee beans and cold or room temperature water in a cold brew coffee maker or jar.
- Let it steep in the refrigerator for 12-24 hours, depending on your desired strength.

Strain Cold Brew:
- After steeping, strain the cold brew concentrate using a fine mesh strainer or cheesecloth into a pitcher.

Mix Honey Lavender Syrup:
- In a small saucepan, heat equal parts honey and water (e.g., 1/2 cup honey and 1/2 cup water) over low heat.
- Add a few drops of lavender syrup to the honey-water mixture.
- Stir until the honey is fully dissolved, and the lavender flavor is infused. Adjust the lavender syrup quantity to your taste.

Assemble Honey Lavender Cold Brew:
- Fill a glass with ice cubes.

- Pour the cold brew concentrate over the ice, leaving room for customization based on your taste preference.
- Drizzle the honey lavender syrup over the cold brew.

Stir and Garnish:
- Stir the cold brew and honey lavender syrup to combine the flavors.
- Optionally, garnish with a few lavender buds for a visual touch.

Serve:
- Serve your Honey Lavender Cold Brew immediately and enjoy the refreshing and aromatic flavor!

Feel free to adjust the sweetness and lavender intensity to suit your taste preferences.

This cold brew variation offers a delightful combination of floral lavender notes and the natural sweetness of honey.

Orange Spice Espresso

Ingredients:

- Freshly brewed espresso (1-2 shots)
- Orange zest (from one orange)
- Ground cinnamon
- Ground nutmeg
- Honey or sweetener of choice (optional)
- Orange slice for garnish (optional)

Equipment:

- Espresso machine
- Zester or grater
- Espresso cup

Instructions:

Brew Espresso:
- Brew 1-2 shots of espresso using your espresso machine.

Prepare Orange Zest:
- Zest the orange using a zester or grater. Be careful to only get the orange part of the peel, avoiding the bitter white pith.

Infuse Orange Zest:
- Sprinkle the freshly brewed espresso with the orange zest while it's still hot. Allow the flavors to infuse for a minute.

Add Spices:
- Sprinkle a pinch of ground cinnamon and ground nutmeg over the infused espresso. Adjust the quantity based on your taste preference.

Optional Sweetener:
- If desired, add honey or your preferred sweetener to the espresso. Stir well to dissolve.

Stir and Garnish:
- Stir the espresso to ensure all the flavors are well combined.
- Optionally, garnish the espresso with a thin slice of orange on the rim of the cup.

Serve:

- Serve your Orange Spice Espresso immediately and savor the warm and aromatic combination of orange and spices.

This Orange Spice Espresso brings a burst of citrusy freshness combined with the warm notes of cinnamon and nutmeg to elevate your espresso experience. Adjust the sweetness and spice levels according to your taste preferences. Enjoy!

Rosemary Infused Coffee

Ingredients:

- Freshly ground coffee beans
- Fresh rosemary sprigs
- Water

Equipment:

- Coffee maker or preferred brewing method
- Coffee grinder
- Coffee filter or reusable filter

Instructions:

Grind Coffee:
- Grind your coffee beans to the coarseness suitable for your chosen brewing method.

Infuse Rosemary:
- Place the ground coffee in your coffee filter or reusable filter.
- Tuck a couple of fresh rosemary sprigs among the coffee grounds.
- Ensure that the rosemary is evenly distributed throughout the coffee.

Brew Coffee:
- Brew your coffee using your preferred method, such as a drip coffee maker, pour-over, or French press.

Allow Infusion:
- Once brewed, let the coffee sit for a minute or two to allow the rosemary flavors to infuse into the coffee.

Strain or Remove Rosemary:
- If using a coffee maker, simply remove the rosemary sprigs from the coffee filter.
- If using a French press, strain the coffee to separate the rosemary.

Serve:
- Pour the rosemary-infused coffee into your mug or cup.

Optional: Garnish (Optional):
- Garnish with a fresh sprig of rosemary on the side of the cup for a visual touch.

Enjoy:

- Sip and enjoy the aromatic and herbal notes of the rosemary-infused coffee.

This Rosemary Infused Coffee offers a unique and aromatic twist to your regular cup of coffee, bringing out the earthy and pine-like flavors of rosemary. Adjust the amount of rose

Cherry Almond Coffee

Ingredients:

- Freshly ground coffee beans
- Cherry syrup or cherry juice
- Almond syrup or almond extract
- Milk (dairy or non-dairy)
- Whipped cream
- Sliced almonds for garnish (optional)
- Chocolate shavings for garnish (optional)

Equipment:

- Coffee maker or preferred brewing method
- Milk frother or steam wand (if making a latte)
- Coffee mug or cup

Instructions:

Brew Coffee:
- Brew a cup of coffee using your preferred method. Make it strong if you enjoy a robust flavor.

Prepare Cherry Almond Syrup:
- In a small bowl, mix cherry syrup or cherry juice with almond syrup or a few drops of almond extract. Adjust the quantities based on your taste preference.

Sweeten Coffee:
- Add the cherry almond syrup mixture to your freshly brewed coffee. Stir well to incorporate the flavors.

Heat Milk (Optional):
- If you prefer a latte, heat and froth your milk using a milk frother or steam wand. Ensure a velvety microfoam is created.

Add Frothed Milk (Optional):
- Pour the frothed milk into the coffee, holding back the foam with a spoon to create a layered effect. If you prefer a regular coffee, you can skip this step.

Optional Garnishes:
- Top your Cherry Almond Coffee with a dollop of whipped cream.

- Garnish with sliced almonds and chocolate shavings for added texture and visual appeal.

Serve:
- Serve your Cherry Almond Coffee hot and enjoy the delightful combination of cherry, almond, and coffee flavors.

This Cherry Almond Coffee is a delightful blend of fruity sweetness and nutty richness, making it a treat for your taste buds. Adjust the sweetness and almond-cherry intensity to suit your preferences.

Horchata Coffee

Ingredients:

For Horchata:

- 1 cup long-grain white rice
- 2 cinnamon sticks
- 3 cups water
- 1 cup milk (dairy or non-dairy)
- 1/2 cup granulated sugar
- 1 teaspoon vanilla extract

For Horchata Coffee:

- Freshly brewed coffee
- Horchata
- Ice cubes
- Ground cinnamon for garnish (optional)

Equipment:

- Blender
- Fine mesh strainer or cheesecloth
- Coffee maker or preferred brewing method
- Glass or cup

Instructions:

Prepare Horchata:

> In a blender, combine the long-grain white rice, cinnamon sticks, and 3 cups of water.
> Blend until the rice and cinnamon are broken down, creating a coarse mixture.
> Let the mixture sit at room temperature for about 3 hours or refrigerate it overnight.

Strain the mixture using a fine mesh strainer or cheesecloth into a bowl, extracting as much liquid as possible.

Return the liquid to the blender and add milk, granulated sugar, and vanilla extract. Blend until well combined.

Strain the mixture again to remove any remaining solids. Your horchata is now ready.

Make Horchata Coffee:

Brew a cup of your favorite coffee using your preferred method.
Fill a glass with ice cubes.
Pour horchata over the ice until the glass is about 3/4 full.
Pour freshly brewed coffee over the horchata.
Stir gently to combine the flavors.
Optionally, sprinkle ground cinnamon on top for garnish.
Serve your refreshing Horchata Coffee and enjoy!

This Horchata Coffee combines the rich and creamy flavors of horchata with the boldness of coffee, creating a delightful and refreshing beverage. Adjust the sweetness and cinnamon to suit your taste preferences.

Coconut Lavender Latte

Ingredients:

For Coconut Lavender Syrup:

- 1 cup coconut milk
- 1/2 cup granulated sugar
- 1 tablespoon dried lavender buds (culinary grade)
- 1 teaspoon vanilla extract

For Coconut Lavender Latte:

- Freshly brewed espresso or strong coffee
- Coconut Lavender Syrup
- Steamed coconut milk
- Dried lavender buds for garnish (optional)

Equipment:

- Saucepan
- Fine mesh strainer or cheesecloth
- Espresso machine or coffee maker
- Milk frother or steam wand
- Latte glass or cup

Instructions:

Prepare Coconut Lavender Syrup:

In a saucepan, combine coconut milk, granulated sugar, dried lavender buds, and vanilla extract.
Heat the mixture over medium heat, stirring frequently until the sugar dissolves.
Bring the mixture to a gentle simmer and let it simmer for about 5 minutes.
Remove the saucepan from heat and let the syrup steep for an additional 10-15 minutes to infuse the lavender flavor.

Strain the syrup using a fine mesh strainer or cheesecloth to remove the lavender buds.
Allow the syrup to cool before using.

Make Coconut Lavender Latte:

Brew a double shot of espresso or a strong cup of coffee using your preferred method.
In a separate container, heat and froth the coconut milk using a milk frother or steam wand until you achieve velvety microfoam.
Pour the freshly brewed espresso into a latte glass or cup.
Add 1-2 tablespoons of the Coconut Lavender Syrup to the espresso, adjusting to your desired sweetness.
Pour the steamed coconut milk over the espresso, holding back the foam with a spoon to create a layered effect.
Stir gently to combine the flavors of the lavender-infused syrup, coconut, and espresso.
Optionally, garnish with a sprinkle of dried lavender buds for aroma and visual appeal.
Serve your Coconut Lavender Latte immediately and enjoy the unique blend of coconut and floral lavender notes.

This Coconut Lavender Latte offers a soothing and aromatic experience with the tropical essence of coconut and the subtle floral undertones of lavender. Adjust the sweetness and lavender intensity to suit your taste preferences.

Spicy Mexican Mocha

Ingredients:

For Spiced Chocolate Sauce:

- 2 tablespoons cocoa powder
- 2 tablespoons sugar
- 1/4 teaspoon ground cinnamon
- 1/8 teaspoon cayenne pepper (adjust to taste)
- 1/2 cup hot water

For Spicy Mexican Mocha:

- Freshly brewed espresso or strong coffee
- Spiced Chocolate Sauce
- Milk (dairy or non-dairy)
- Whipped cream for topping
- Ground cinnamon for garnish

Equipment:

- Small bowl
- Whisk or spoon
- Saucepan
- Espresso machine or coffee maker
- Milk frother or steam wand
- Latte glass or cup

Instructions:

Prepare Spiced Chocolate Sauce:

In a small bowl, whisk together cocoa powder, sugar, ground cinnamon, and cayenne pepper.
Heat 1/2 cup of hot water in a saucepan.

Gradually whisk the cocoa mixture into the hot water, ensuring it is well combined.
Bring the mixture to a gentle simmer, stirring continuously until it thickens slightly.
Remove from heat and set aside.

Make Spicy Mexican Mocha:

Brew a double shot of espresso or a strong cup of coffee using your preferred method.
Froth the milk using a milk frother or steam wand until you achieve velvety microfoam.
In a latte glass or cup, combine the freshly brewed espresso and 2-3 tablespoons of the Spiced Chocolate Sauce. Adjust the amount based on your desired level of chocolatey spice.
Pour the frothed milk over the espresso and chocolate mixture, holding back the foam with a spoon to create a layered effect.
Stir gently to combine the flavors.
Top with whipped cream for a creamy finish.
Sprinkle ground cinnamon on top for garnish.
Serve your Spicy Mexican Mocha immediately and savor the rich, spicy, and chocolaty notes.

This Spicy Mexican Mocha adds a kick to your traditional mocha with the warmth of cinnamon and a hint of cayenne pepper. Adjust the level of spice according to your taste preferences for a unique and invigorating coffee experience.

Dessert-Inspired Coffees:

Tiramisu Latte

Ingredients:

For Tiramisu Syrup:

- 1/2 cup strong brewed coffee
- 1/2 cup granulated sugar
- 1 tablespoon unsweetened cocoa powder
- 1 teaspoon vanilla extract
- 1 tablespoon mascarpone cheese

For Tiramisu Latte:

- Freshly brewed espresso or strong coffee
- Tiramisu Syrup
- Steamed milk (whole milk or your choice)
- Whipped cream for topping
- Cocoa powder for garnish

Equipment:

- Saucepan
- Whisk or spoon
- Espresso machine or coffee maker
- Milk frother or steam wand
- Latte glass or cup

Instructions:

Prepare Tiramisu Syrup:

In a saucepan, combine strong brewed coffee, granulated sugar, cocoa powder, vanilla extract, and mascarpone cheese.

Heat the mixture over medium heat, stirring continuously until the sugar and mascarpone cheese are fully dissolved.
Bring the mixture to a gentle simmer, allowing it to thicken slightly.
Remove from heat and set aside.

Make Tiramisu Latte:

Brew a double shot of espresso or a strong cup of coffee using your preferred method.
Froth the milk using a milk frother or steam wand until you achieve velvety microfoam.
In a latte glass or cup, combine the freshly brewed espresso and 2-3 tablespoons of the Tiramisu Syrup. Adjust the amount based on your desired sweetness.
Pour the frothed milk over the espresso and syrup mixture, holding back the foam with a spoon to create a layered effect.
Stir gently to combine the flavors.
Top with whipped cream for a luxurious finish.
Dust cocoa powder on top for garnish.
Serve your Tiramisu Latte immediately and enjoy the delightful blend of coffee and the classic flavors of tiramisu.

This Tiramisu Latte brings the beloved Italian dessert into your coffee cup, combining the richness of mascarpone, the sweetness of vanilla, and the boldness of coffee. Adjust the sweetness and mascarpone intensity to suit your taste preferences for a delicious treat.

Chocolate Cheesecake Coffee

Ingredients:

For Chocolate Cheesecake Syrup:

- 1/4 cup cream cheese, softened
- 2 tablespoons unsweetened cocoa powder
- 1/4 cup chocolate syrup
- 1/4 cup sugar
- 1/2 cup milk (dairy or non-dairy)
- 1/2 teaspoon vanilla extract

For Chocolate Cheesecake Coffee:

- Freshly brewed espresso or strong coffee
- Chocolate Cheesecake Syrup
- Steamed milk (whole milk or your choice)
- Whipped cream for topping
- Chocolate shavings for garnish

Equipment:

- Saucepan
- Whisk or spoon
- Espresso machine or coffee maker
- Milk frother or steam wand
- Latte glass or cup

Instructions:

Prepare Chocolate Cheesecake Syrup:

In a saucepan, combine softened cream cheese, cocoa powder, chocolate syrup, sugar, milk, and vanilla extract.
Heat the mixture over medium heat, whisking continuously until the cream cheese is fully melted and the ingredients are well combined.
Bring the mixture to a gentle simmer, allowing it to thicken slightly.
Remove from heat and set aside.

Make Chocolate Cheesecake Coffee:

- Brew a double shot of espresso or a strong cup of coffee using your preferred method.
- Froth the milk using a milk frother or steam wand until you achieve velvety microfoam.
- In a latte glass or cup, combine the freshly brewed espresso and 2-3 tablespoons of the Chocolate Cheesecake Syrup. Adjust the amount based on your desired sweetness.
- Pour the frothed milk over the espresso and syrup mixture, holding back the foam with a spoon to create a layered effect.
- Stir gently to combine the flavors.
- Top with whipped cream for a decadent finish.
- Garnish with chocolate shavings on top.
- Serve your Chocolate Cheesecake Coffee immediately and indulge in the rich and creamy flavors.

This Chocolate Cheesecake Coffee is a delightful combination of chocolate, cream cheese, and coffee, reminiscent of the classic dessert. Adjust the sweetness and creaminess to suit your taste preferences for a luscious coffee treat.

Crème Brûlée Coffee

Ingredients:

For Vanilla Custard Cream:

- 1 cup heavy cream
- 1 cup whole milk
- 1/2 cup granulated sugar
- 4 large egg yolks
- 2 teaspoons vanilla extract

For Crème Brûlée Coffee:

- Freshly brewed espresso or strong coffee
- Vanilla Custard Cream
- Whipped cream for topping
- Brown sugar for caramelizing
- Fresh berries for garnish (optional)

Equipment:

- Saucepan
- Whisk or spoon
- Mixing bowls
- Espresso machine or coffee maker
- Blowtorch or kitchen torch
- Latte glass or cup

Instructions:

Prepare Vanilla Custard Cream:

In a saucepan, heat the heavy cream and whole milk over medium heat until it begins to simmer. Do not boil.
In a mixing bowl, whisk together sugar and egg yolks until well combined.
Slowly pour the warm milk mixture into the egg mixture, whisking continuously to prevent curdling.
Return the combined mixture to the saucepan and heat over medium-low heat, stirring constantly until it thickens to coat the back of a spoon.

Remove from heat, strain the custard to remove any lumps, and stir in vanilla extract.

Allow the custard to cool before refrigerating for at least 2 hours or until chilled.

Make Crème Brûlée Coffee:

Brew a double shot of espresso or a strong cup of coffee using your preferred method.

In a latte glass or cup, pour a generous amount of the chilled Vanilla Custard Cream.

Pour the freshly brewed espresso over the custard cream, stirring gently to combine.

Top the coffee with whipped cream for a luxurious finish.

Sprinkle a layer of brown sugar evenly over the whipped cream.

Using a blowtorch or kitchen torch, caramelize the sugar until it forms a crispy, golden crust.

Garnish with fresh berries if desired.

Serve your Crème Brûlée Coffee immediately and savor the decadent and indulgent flavors.

This Crème Brûlée Coffee captures the essence of the classic dessert with rich custard and a perfectly caramelized sugar crust. Adjust the sweetness and caramelization level to suit your taste preferences for a delightful coffee experience.

Pumpkin Spice Latte

Ingredients:

For Pumpkin Spice Syrup:

- 1/2 cup canned pumpkin puree
- 1/2 cup granulated sugar
- 1/2 cup water
- 1 teaspoon pumpkin spice blend (cinnamon, nutmeg, ginger, cloves)
- 1 teaspoon vanilla extract

For Pumpkin Spice Latte:

- Freshly brewed espresso or strong coffee
- Pumpkin Spice Syrup
- Steamed milk (whole milk or your choice)
- Whipped cream for topping
- Pumpkin spice blend for garnish

Equipment:

- Saucepan
- Whisk or spoon
- Espresso machine or coffee maker
- Milk frother or steam wand
- Latte glass or cup

Instructions:

Prepare Pumpkin Spice Syrup:

In a saucepan, combine canned pumpkin puree, granulated sugar, water, pumpkin spice blend, and vanilla extract.
Heat the mixture over medium heat, whisking continuously until the sugar is fully dissolved.
Bring the mixture to a gentle simmer, allowing it to thicken slightly.
Remove from heat and set aside.

Make Pumpkin Spice Latte:

Brew a double shot of espresso or a strong cup of coffee using your preferred method.

Froth the milk using a milk frother or steam wand until you achieve velvety microfoam.

In a latte glass or cup, combine the freshly brewed espresso and 2-3 tablespoons of the Pumpkin Spice Syrup. Adjust the amount based on your desired sweetness.

Pour the frothed milk over the espresso and syrup mixture, holding back the foam with a spoon to create a layered effect.

Stir gently to combine the flavors.

Top with whipped cream for a decadent finish.

Sprinkle a pinch of pumpkin spice blend on top for garnish.

Serve your Pumpkin Spice Latte immediately and enjoy the warm and comforting flavors of fall.

This Pumpkin Spice Latte is a seasonal favorite, capturing the essence of autumn with the warmth of pumpkin and aromatic spices. Adjust the sweetness and spice level to suit your taste preferences for a cozy and delicious coffee treat.

Chocolate Covered Strawberry Coffee

Ingredients:

For Strawberry Syrup:

- 1 cup fresh strawberries, hulled and chopped
- 1/2 cup granulated sugar
- 1/2 cup water
- 1 teaspoon lemon juice

For Chocolate Covered Strawberry Coffee:

- Freshly brewed espresso or strong coffee
- Strawberry Syrup
- Chocolate syrup
- Steamed milk (whole milk or your choice)
- Whipped cream for topping
- Fresh strawberries for garnish

Equipment:

- Saucepan
- Blender or immersion blender
- Fine mesh strainer or cheesecloth
- Espresso machine or coffee maker
- Milk frother or steam wand
- Latte glass or cup

Instructions:

Prepare Strawberry Syrup:

In a saucepan, combine chopped strawberries, granulated sugar, water, and lemon juice.
Heat the mixture over medium heat, stirring occasionally until the strawberries break down and the sugar is fully dissolved.

Bring the mixture to a gentle simmer, allowing it to thicken.
Remove from heat and let it cool for a few minutes.
Use a blender or immersion blender to puree the mixture until smooth.
Strain the syrup using a fine mesh strainer or cheesecloth to remove seeds and pulp.
Set the strawberry syrup aside.

Make Chocolate Covered Strawberry Coffee:

Brew a double shot of espresso or a strong cup of coffee using your preferred method.
In a latte glass or cup, combine the freshly brewed espresso, 2-3 tablespoons of Strawberry Syrup, and a drizzle of chocolate syrup. Adjust the amounts based on your desired sweetness.
Froth the milk using a milk frother or steam wand until you achieve velvety microfoam.
Pour the frothed milk over the espresso and syrups, holding back the foam with a spoon to create a layered effect.
Stir gently to combine the flavors.
Top with whipped cream for a luscious finish.
Drizzle a bit more chocolate syrup on top.
Garnish with fresh strawberries.

Serve your Chocolate Covered Strawberry Coffee immediately and revel in the delightful combination of rich chocolate, sweet strawberries, and bold coffee. Adjust the sweetness and chocolate-to-strawberry ratio according to your taste preferences.

Bananas Foster Coffee

Ingredients:

For Bananas Foster Sauce:

- 2 ripe bananas, sliced
- 1/4 cup unsalted butter
- 1/2 cup brown sugar, packed
- 1/4 cup dark rum
- 1/2 teaspoon ground cinnamon
- 1/4 teaspoon vanilla extract

For Bananas Foster Coffee:

- Freshly brewed espresso or strong coffee
- Bananas Foster Sauce
- Steamed milk (whole milk or your choice)
- Whipped cream for topping
- Caramel sauce for drizzling
- Banana slices for garnish

Equipment:

- Saucepan
- Whisk or spoon
- Espresso machine or coffee maker
- Milk frother or steam wand
- Latte glass or cup

Instructions:

Prepare Bananas Foster Sauce:

In a saucepan, melt the butter over medium heat.
Add the sliced bananas, brown sugar, dark rum, ground cinnamon, and vanilla extract.

Cook the mixture, stirring occasionally, until the bananas are softened and the sauce is caramelized.

Be cautious as the alcohol in the rum may flame. If desired, you can flambe the sauce by carefully igniting it with a long lighter.

Make Bananas Foster Coffee:

Brew a double shot of espresso or a strong cup of coffee using your preferred method.

In a latte glass or cup, combine the freshly brewed espresso and 2-3 tablespoons of the Bananas Foster Sauce.

Froth the milk using a milk frother or steam wand until you achieve velvety microfoam.

Pour the frothed milk over the espresso and Bananas Foster Sauce, holding back the foam with a spoon to create a layered effect.

Stir gently to combine the flavors.

Top with whipped cream for a decadent finish.

Drizzle caramel sauce over the whipped cream.

Garnish with banana slices.

Serve your Bananas Foster Coffee immediately and savor the rich and caramelized flavors inspired by the classic New Orleans dessert. Adjust the sweetness and banana-rum intensity to suit your taste preferences.

Salted Caramel Affogato

Ingredients:

For Salted Caramel Sauce:

- 1 cup granulated sugar
- 1/4 cup water
- 1/2 cup heavy cream
- 4 tablespoons unsalted butter
- 1 teaspoon sea salt (adjust to taste)

For Salted Caramel Affogato:

- Vanilla bean ice cream or gelato
- Freshly brewed espresso or strong coffee
- Salted Caramel Sauce
- Sea salt flakes for garnish

Equipment:

- Saucepan
- Whisk or spoon
- Espresso machine or coffee maker
- Ice cream scoop
- Dessert glass or cup

Instructions:

Prepare Salted Caramel Sauce:

In a saucepan, combine granulated sugar and water over medium heat, stirring until the sugar dissolves.
Once the sugar has dissolved, stop stirring and let it simmer until it turns a deep amber color. Swirl the pan occasionally to ensure even caramelization.
Carefully add the heavy cream while continuously whisking to combine.
Remove the saucepan from heat and stir in the unsalted butter until smooth.

Add sea salt, adjusting to your desired level of saltiness.
Allow the salted caramel sauce to cool before using.

Make Salted Caramel Affogato:

Scoop a generous portion of vanilla bean ice cream or gelato into a dessert glass or cup.
Brew a double shot of espresso or a strong cup of coffee using your preferred method.
Pour the freshly brewed espresso over the scoops of ice cream.
Drizzle the Salted Caramel Sauce over the ice cream and espresso.
Garnish with a sprinkle of sea salt flakes for an extra touch of saltiness.
Serve your Salted Caramel Affogato immediately and enjoy the delightful combination of hot espresso melting the ice cream, complemented by the rich salted caramel.

This Salted Caramel Affogato is a luxurious and indulgent dessert coffee, combining the warmth of espresso with the cool creaminess of vanilla ice cream, all bathed in a luscious salted caramel sauce. Adjust the saltiness and caramel sweetness according to your taste preferences.

Cinnamon Roll Latte

Ingredients:

For Cinnamon Roll Syrup:

- 1/4 cup unsalted butter
- 1/4 cup brown sugar, packed
- 1/4 cup maple syrup
- 1 teaspoon ground cinnamon
- 1/2 teaspoon vanilla extract

For Cinnamon Roll Latte:

- Freshly brewed espresso or strong coffee
- Cinnamon Roll Syrup
- Steamed milk (whole milk or your choice)
- Whipped cream for topping
- Ground cinnamon for garnish

Equipment:

- Saucepan
- Whisk or spoon
- Espresso machine or coffee maker
- Milk frother or steam wand
- Latte glass or cup

Instructions:

Prepare Cinnamon Roll Syrup:

    In a saucepan, melt the unsalted butter over medium heat.
    Add brown sugar, maple syrup, ground cinnamon, and vanilla extract.
    Stir the mixture until the sugar is dissolved, and the syrup is well combined.
    Allow the syrup to simmer for a few minutes until it thickens slightly.
    Remove from heat and set aside.

Make Cinnamon Roll Latte:

Brew a double shot of espresso or a strong cup of coffee using your preferred method.

In a latte glass or cup, combine the freshly brewed espresso and 2-3 tablespoons of the Cinnamon Roll Syrup. Adjust the amount based on your desired sweetness.

Froth the milk using a milk frother or steam wand until you achieve velvety microfoam.

Pour the frothed milk over the espresso and syrup mixture, holding back the foam with a spoon to create a layered effect.

Stir gently to combine the flavors.

Top with whipped cream for a decadent finish.

Sprinkle ground cinnamon on top for garnish.

Serve your Cinnamon Roll Latte immediately and relish the comforting and sweet notes reminiscent of a freshly baked cinnamon roll.

This Cinnamon Roll Latte brings the delightful flavors of cinnamon, sugar, and vanilla into your coffee, creating a cozy and indulgent beverage. Adjust the sweetness and cinnamon intensity to suit your taste preferences for a delightful treat.

Blueberry Cobbler Coffee

Ingredients:

For Blueberry Cobbler Syrup:

- 1 cup fresh blueberries
- 1/2 cup granulated sugar
- 1/2 cup water
- 1 teaspoon lemon juice
- 1/2 teaspoon vanilla extract
- 1/4 teaspoon ground cinnamon

For Blueberry Cobbler Coffee:

- Freshly brewed espresso or strong coffee
- Blueberry Cobbler Syrup
- Steamed milk (whole milk or your choice)
- Whipped cream for topping
- Fresh blueberries for garnish

Equipment:

- Saucepan
- Whisk or spoon
- Fine mesh strainer or cheesecloth
- Espresso machine or coffee maker
- Milk frother or steam wand
- Latte glass or cup

Instructions:

Prepare Blueberry Cobbler Syrup:

In a saucepan, combine fresh blueberries, granulated sugar, water, lemon juice, vanilla extract, and ground cinnamon.

Heat the mixture over medium heat, stirring occasionally until the blueberries break down and the sugar is fully dissolved.

Bring the mixture to a gentle simmer, allowing it to thicken slightly.

Remove from heat and let it cool for a few minutes.

Use a fine mesh strainer or cheesecloth to strain the syrup, separating the liquid from the blueberry solids.

Set the blueberry syrup aside.

Make Blueberry Cobbler Coffee:

Brew a double shot of espresso or a strong cup of coffee using your preferred method.

In a latte glass or cup, combine the freshly brewed espresso and 2-3 tablespoons of the Blueberry Cobbler Syrup. Adjust the amount based on your desired sweetness.

Froth the milk using a milk frother or steam wand until you achieve velvety microfoam.

Pour the frothed milk over the espresso and syrup mixture, holding back the foam with a spoon to create a layered effect.

Stir gently to combine the flavors.

Top with whipped cream for a decadent finish.

Garnish with fresh blueberries on top.

Serve your Blueberry Cobbler Coffee immediately and enjoy the delightful taste of blueberries with a hint of cinnamon in your coffee.

This Blueberry Cobbler Coffee captures the essence of a classic dessert in a comforting and flavorful drink. Adjust the sweetness and blueberry intensity to suit your taste preferences for a delightful treat.

Eggnog Latte

Ingredients:

For Eggnog Syrup:

- 1 cup eggnog
- 1/4 cup granulated sugar
- 1/2 teaspoon ground nutmeg
- 1/2 teaspoon vanilla extract

For Eggnog Latte:

- Freshly brewed espresso or strong coffee
- Eggnog Syrup
- Steamed eggnog (whole eggnog or your choice)
- Whipped cream for topping
- Ground nutmeg for garnish

Equipment:

- Saucepan
- Whisk or spoon
- Espresso machine or coffee maker
- Milk frother or steam wand
- Latte glass or cup

Instructions:

Prepare Eggnog Syrup:

In a saucepan, combine eggnog, granulated sugar, ground nutmeg, and vanilla extract.
Heat the mixture over medium heat, stirring occasionally until the sugar is fully dissolved.
Bring the mixture to a gentle simmer, allowing it to thicken slightly.
Remove from heat and set aside.

Make Eggnog Latte:

Brew a double shot of espresso or a strong cup of coffee using your preferred method.

In a latte glass or cup, combine the freshly brewed espresso and 2-3 tablespoons of the Eggnog Syrup. Adjust the amount based on your desired sweetness.

Froth the eggnog using a milk frother or steam wand until you achieve velvety microfoam.

Pour the frothed eggnog over the espresso and syrup mixture, holding back the foam with a spoon to create a layered effect.

Stir gently to combine the flavors.

Top with whipped cream for a festive finish.

Sprinkle ground nutmeg on top for garnish.

Serve your Eggnog Latte immediately and enjoy the rich and holiday-inspired flavors.

This Eggnog Latte brings the warmth and spice of the holiday season into your coffee cup. Adjust the sweetness and nutmeg intensity to suit your taste preferences for a cozy and festive coffee experience.

www.ingramcontent.com/pod-product-compliance
Lightning Source LLC
LaVergne TN
LVHW081613060526
838201LV00054B/2225